Big Al's Turbo MLM

by
Tom Schreiter

KAAS Publishing
P.O. Box 890084
Houston, TX 77289
(713) 280-9800

Cover Design: Eric Gignac

About the author

Tom "Big Al" Schreiter was once a popular speaker to multilevel groups. His audiences left his lectures with confidence in their future success in multilevel. This is best exemplified by their comments, "If he can do it, anybody can do it!"

As word of his lectures spread throughout the multi-level industry, his bookings quickly stopped. Distributors would plead, "Please don't speak to our group. Just send us information in the mail. Don't call us, we'll call you."

So in response to this universal groundswell for information in the mail, this book was written.

The author has also written three other books whose commercials are prominently displayed in the back of this book.

Table of Contents

Sponsor by mail

"$50 per thousand! That's highway robbery!" Distributor Joe didn't want the mailing list broker on the other end of the phone to think he was some amateur.

"I have a flyer in front of me right now that's offering prime opportunity seekers for only $15 per thousand. And you know why they're so cheap? Because this flyer is on cheap, seventh generation photocopied paper instead of your overpriced glossy brochure. I'm not going to have you rip me off with expensive names. Call me when you can produce mailing lists at rock bottom prices."

After hanging up the phone, Joe thought, "I'm really a pretty sharp operator. So what if that list broker has 20 years experience, I know what I'm doing. Just think, I'm getting three times as many names by buying from this mail order flyer. Retirement City – here I come."

Joe was going to make multilevel history with his "foolproof" mail order recruiting campaign. The multilevel pros would watch with amazement as Joe recruited thousands of prospects right under their noses. There could be a banquet thrown in Joe's honor for revolutionizing multilevel recruiting techniques. Maybe they would put his statue in the MLM Hall of Fame?

How could Joe lose? Every piece of his three-part master plan was in place.

1. The list.

Joe would rent 50,000 names of opportunity seekers from his bargain basement list seller. Normally, mailing lists cost $50 per thousand, but by buying an old list, Joe had cut the cost to one third paying only $15 per thousand. Total cost for the list rental? Only $750, well within Joe's master plan budget.

2. The mail package.

Why pay an expensive copywriter when Joe knew what the prospect wanted to hear? Most copywriters are not familiar with multilevel, so Joe was the best choice. Joe carefully reviewed the multilevel mail offers he had received over the past year. With enthusiastic prose, Joe produced a wonderful four-page sales letter. Joe's girlfriend copied the four-page sales letter during her lunch hour at work. It only took three months. His girlfriend's employer would never notice the extra 50,000 copies on the copy machine, and it saved several thousand dollars in printing costs.

Next, Joe purchased 50,000 company brochures at 15 cents each (total cost: $7,500). The slick appearance of his company's brochure would add a touch of class to the mailing.

Finally, a postage-paid return envelope completed the package.

3. Postage.

No way to get around the government. The cost of 50,000 stamps at 29 cents each was $14,500. Sure it would be cheaper by bulk rate, but that's junk mail. Joe wanted his mailing to work.

By watching his budget, Joe was sure his mail order recruiting program would be a success.

The total cost:

$14,500	postage
7,500	company brochures
750	mailing list rental
750	postage paid return envelopes
120	doctor visit*
5	stress tabs
85	dinner, flowers**

$23,710

*Joe got sick licking 50,000 stamps.
**Repair relationship with girlfriend.

The hardest part of the entire project was the labor to stuff, stamp, label, and seal 50,000 packets. Joe used his two week vacation for the project. Why worry about using his vacation time as in only a few weeks, money would be pouring into his mailbox? Joe wouldn't need his full-time job then.

A quick second mortgage on Joe's house provided the capital needed for this journey into MLM mail-order riches. Was a $20,000 second mortgage risky? Joe knew it wasn't. At least 1,000 new distributors would sign up from his mailings. Everyone knows that mail order gets a 2 percent response. With 50,000 packets out in the mail, the 2 percent return would mean 1,000 new distributors. Those 1,000 new distributors would each sign up two or three new distributors, who would each sign up a few distributors, and soon Joe would have the largest group ever assembled in multilevel marketing history.

"I gotta face it," Joe thought. "I'm an idea man. Some people are plodders; some follow proven paths; I blaze new trails with my innovative ideas. Those distributors of lesser caliber can follow humbly in my footsteps."

Why worry about a temporary second mortgage? The 1,000 new distributors would earn Joe so much money, he'd have to purchase a larger house for his new millionaire image.

The returns are in

One week later, Joe lay in his favorite lawn chair awaiting the mailman. He wanted to make sure the neighbors noticed him receiving the bag of checks he expected shortly.

Just as he predicted, here came the mailman with two large mailbags in a mail cart.

"Here you are, Joe. You're sure popular today."

Joe quickly lugged the bags inside. "I'd better be careful opening envelopes stuffed with checks. Maybe I should have hired a security guard."

He dumped the first bag on the floor. "Hey! These envelopes look familiar. They are the same ones I mailed out last week!"

The entire bag contained the original envelopes with yellow stickers saying, "Return to Sender." "Moved." "Forwarding order expired." "Address unknown."

The second bag contained more undelivered envelopes. "There must be a thousand of these returns," moaned Joe.

The next day was worse. Another bag of returned envelopes depressed Joe even more. "I can't believe this. I have over 40 cents invested in each envelope. Look at the money I have wasted!"

And so the week continued.

"Maybe I should have invested more money in a better list. The extra cost would only be a fraction of what I've wasted on these returned envelopes. Next time will be different." Joe talked to himself a lot during the past week.

"How could so many people move? The list broker said people only move at the rate of 10-20% a year. This list must be from the Civil War. Cheap mailing lists are expensive. I haven't received a single reply yet. I used postage paid return envelopes. Maybe next week I'll receive some replies."

Monday morning Joe overslept and missed the mailman. When he opened his mailbox there was a notice to come to the Post Office. Some of his business reply envelopes had finally come back. Sure, he would have to pay the return postage on each, but the replies would be stuffed with checks. "Ah, the thrill of victory. So what if there are a bunch of returns? It is the end result that counts. I guess I became depressed too soon," thought Joe. "Patience is a virtue. I wonder if a rented limousine or an armored car is proper transportation for my trip?"

Joe drove his own car. He couldn't wait to pick up his responses. Opening envelopes with checks would make him forget the dread of seeing the evil words "Return to Sender."

"Next," announced the clerk. Joe gave her his notice and she returned his mail. "What a stack!" thought Joe. "There must be 400 replies!"

"That will be $150 for your return postage," said the clerk.

Joe quickly wrote the check to redeem his replies and stuffed the replies in his car. "Better open these at home. Can't be too careful nowadays."

Joe's troubles were just beginning.

The first five envelopes were empty. "There are some rude and sick people out there. They must get pleasure having me pay for their empty envelopes."

The next batch of envelopes contained mail order solicitations from other mailers. "Can you believe it? These people use my envelopes to send me their offers. I have to pay the postage and they expect me to buy from them? Those cheapies have dog droppings on their brains."

Some more envelopes had multilevel offers from other distributors. "I can't believe these people. I invest $20,000 in a mailing and they think I'll throw it all away and join them? What kind of attitude do they think I'll have when I have to pay the postage for their cheap efforts?"

The balance of envelopes had chain letters. "Send $5 to each of the four names listed. Don't break the chain or something terrible will happen to you. I know somebody who heard of a person who knew a person who might have become rich doing this, etc."

"I didn't know there was such a variety of chain letters," thought Joe. "There are chain letters for recipes, reports, stamps, embroidery, good vibes, and mailing lists. I think the world's I.Q. has dropped 50 points since I made my mailing."

The next day, Joe redeemed another $100 worth of postage-paid reply envelopes from the post office. "I can't afford to keep redeeming these insults," whined Joe. "I can't afford not to redeem them either. It's my only possible source of prospects from my $20,000 investment. I wonder how I'm going to pay off my second mortgage?"

Play the odds

"There are no shortcuts to success." Big Al was consoling Distributor Joe. "You can't buy success in multilevel either."

Joe didn't want a lecture. He wanted answers.

"I know I have to go back recruiting the sure way, two-on-one. That's the only way I'll pay back my second mortgage. What I want to know is what I did wrong in my mailing campaign. Don't tell me that I should buy better lists. I know that already."

"Okay, Joe. Grab your pencil."

Play a game where the odds are on your side.

"You stepped into an arena against some pretty stiff competition. Professional mailers spend thousands of dollars creating, testing, and producing high-class mailing packages. Are you any match for an $80,000-a-year full-time copywriter with 20 years experience?"

"No."

"Do you have an in-house list consultant to evaluate and choose your mailing list?"

"No."

"Did you test different models of your mailing package and compare pulling power?"

"No." Joe began to feel ill.

"Were your stickmen any competition against a $50,000-a-year graphics designer?"

"No."

"Did your photocopied package stick out in a stack of full color packages from your competition?"

"Yes, but not favorably."

"So you see, Joe, it takes some money to play in the big leagues."

"The Big Leagues"

"The good news is that you only received a few unqualified replies."

"That's the good news?" Joe gasped.

"Sure is. Saved you a lot of money."

"I lost over $20,000 and you tell me I was lucky to get a lousy return?"

"Joe, consider this. What if a John Doe in Maine joined as your first level? He's 1,500 miles away. The long distance phone bills would add up in a hurry. Shipping costs of products or support material cost money. If he is brand new to the business, who will help him do two-on-ones? Airfare alone would make you wish he had never responded. It gets worse."

"What if John Doe calls you, collect of course, and says he has a meeting scheduled? Since he is brand new, shy, and on your first level, who will give the meeting? John will assure you a room full of people. He knows everyone in town will be there to hear you speak. You step off the plane and John tells you he promoted the meeting with ads on the local radio station. The rest is up to you."

"I can finish that story," said Joe. "I've had those kinds of disasters locally. The meeting room will be empty and John Doe won't have any appointments, right?"

"Right, Joe. If you are going to waste your money on mailing, at least waste a mailing looking for self-supporting leaders. Since they are as rare as hen's teeth, you'll need a bigger second mortgage to find them."

"You can't expect someone to read your letter, go spastic, send money to you and the company, and sponsor the entire neighborhood."

"Everyone wants the easy way out. Most new distributors think that becoming a professional stamp-licker will make their business easy. You can't expect someone to read your letter, go spastic, send money to you, the company, and sponsor his entire neighborhood. All you have with a response is just a lead – nothing more. You still have to train, motivate, lead, support, and work hard with your prospect. There are no shortcuts."

"I have about 20,000 reasons why I should never do a mailing again. However, just for conversation, if you had to do a mailing, what would you do differently?" Joe didn't want his mailing idea to die.

"Joe, if I had to waste my money, I'd do it locally. At least it would help the local economy. Seriously, I would mail only within a short drive of my house. Then if someone responded, I could work with him like I would any other distributor. No long distance phone calls, no airfare, no 1,500 mile support problems. But I leave mailing campaigns to the full-time professionals. They have a hard enough time breaking even on large investments, so why should I spend years of my life learning how to break even?"

"Everyone wants a nationwide organization. It's like they believe they saturated their hometown because they live there. Joe, do you know what people in Seattle do?"

"No."

"They mail thousands of recruiting letters to people in Miami. They feel they can expand their income with a Miami group. Do you know what people in Miami do?"

"Mail to Seattle prospects?" guessed Joe.

"Right. Once you see the big picture, it's like the grass is always greener on the other side of the fence. Most amateur multilevel distributors live by that cliche. Don't fall into that trap. Let your competition believe the only way they can expand their income is to waste money outside their hometowns."

"Well, Big Al, I can't spend any more time talking with you. Let's get out of here and do some two-on-ones." Joe's first payment on his second mortgage was due tomorrow.

Don't be fooled

What's the biggest multilevel/mail order myth going?

An average mailing will bring about a two percent return.

What's the stupidest statement in multilevel/mail order?

An average mailing will bring about a two percent return.

Sometime in every multilevel distributor's career, he'll hear the *Two Percent Myth*. If taken at face value, the distributor will spend thousands of dollars on mailings. Why not? It takes only 100 letters to get two new distributors, right?

Wrong.

There is no average return percentage in mail order because there is no average mail offer.

Successful mailings of high-ticket merchandise may need only 1/4 of one percent response. Other offers may need up to four or five percent response just to begin recouping production costs.

The percentage return from your mail order offer will depend on many factors. Here are just a few:

1. Who are you mailing to?

If you rented an opportunity seekers' list, your mailing may be only one of 50 pieces of mail that person receives the day it arrives. You could end up being just another piece of junk mail.

Are you mailing to qualifed buyers or qualified lookers? How was your mailing list compiled? Are you mailing to the right people? If you are offering an entrepreneur home study course to union leaders, you have problems.

2. What does your offer say?

How much have you invested in a professional copywriter and design person? If you mail 17th generation photocopies, you will be hard pressed to get a two percent return even if you are giving away free money!

Are you asking for money or only asking for a response? A lot more people will respond if it doesn't cost them any money. This alone would blow the two percent theory.

Is it easy for your prospect to respond? More people will dial a toll-free phone number than will look for an envelope and make a trip to the post office to write you.

3. Do you know what you are doing?

A full-time, professional mailer would surely get a higher percentage return than a first-time amateur. It's ridiculous to believe both would get an identical two percent return.

So when some "pro" tells you that you can get a two percent return on your mailing, run like heck in the opposite direction and put your hand over your wallet.

Goals must be specific

Once upon a time, a young lady visited an antique shop. While browsing, she noticed a beautiful mirror. When told that the price was $5,000, the young lady gasped. "How could this mirror, lovely as it is, be worth $5,000?"

The shop owner replied, "This is a magic mirror. Look into the mirror, make a wish, and your wish will come true."

Satisfied, the young lady took the magic mirror home and proudly showed her purchase to her husband.

"$5,000 for a mirror! You must be out of your mind!" screamed her husband. "Let's see a demonstration of your stupid mirror."

The young lady stepped in front of the mirror and said, "Mirror, Mirror, on the wall. I wish for a beautiful, full-length mink coat." Instantly, a beautiful, full-length mink coat appeared on her shoulders. She turned to her husband, smirked, and left to show her neighbors the new coat.

The husband looked around and saw no one watching. He stepped in front of the mirror and said, "Mirror, Mirror, on the wall. Make me irresistible to women!"

Instantly, the mirror turned the husband into a bottle of perfume.

Vague goals can be dangerous. Even some long term goals lack day-to-day focus. Performing specific goals and activities daily separates leaders from distributors. Do you have distributors in your group who have vague goals such as:

To get more distributors in my group?

To sponsor more people?

To make manager?

If your group makes vague goals such as these, help them concentrate on revising their goals to specific day-to-day activities.

Sorting for leaders

While there are many ways to divide and subdivide people into groups, let's examine a simple way to sort for leaders.

For recruiting, training, and business-building purposes, it is advantageous for us to categorize people into two groups:

Group One

Those people looking for reasons **WHY** something will work.

Group Two

Those people looking for reasons **WHY NOT**.

Group One individuals are fun to work with. They are mature enough to realize that life isn't perfect. In fact, in many of their business decisions, they acknowledge there may be thousands of reasons *why something won't work.* All they need to go into action is one good reason *why it will work.*

They may be aware that their upline sponsor is a jerk, their personal contacts are useless wimps, the company's logo is the wrong color, the delivery of product is sporadic, the local meetings are boring, etc., but if they have just one good reason *why the opportunity is good* (such as the marketing plan is neat, the product really helps people, etc.), then they can go ahead and be successful in the business.

Group One individuals are not excuse-driven. They look for the positive reasons why something will work, and then go into action.

Group Two individuals are constantly looking for flaws. Why? If they can find the slightest excuse or reason *why something may not work*, they can then justify not trying. They may investigate an opportunity and find thousands of reasons why it will work, but they will concentrate on searching for any little reason not to go into action.

Group Two individuals are people who won't leave the house in the morning unless they can be sure every stoplight on the way to work will be green. Many upline leaders frustrate themselves by attempting to fix every excuse their Group Two distributor can think of. No matter how many obstacles you clear from a Group Two's path, your Group Two distributor will create more to take their place. Their motto is: *Any excuse will do.*

So how's your group? Is it mostly Group One or Group Two people? If you have too many distributors who fall into Group Two, have you considered transferring them to your competition? Professional recruiters encourage their whiners and complainers to look for another opportunity. When the malcontents join the competition, they occupy the competition's time and efforts. Then, the professional recruiters can be first to contact prospects who want to be leaders.

So, what takes more effort? Searching for a Group One prospect or spending a lifetime trying to change a Group Two distributor into a winner?

Closing for Dollars

"You multilevel wimps make me sick," explained Sleaze Shallowman to Distributor Joe. "You go around begging for distributors. A real salesman sells and makes the big bucks. You guys are just a bunch of order takers."

Distributor Joe had just met the ultimate Heavy Hitter, the pro of pros, Sleaze Shallowman. Sleaze had spent the better part of an hour listing his many multilevel accomplishments. As a distributor with eight different companies over the past two years, Sleaze shared how he broke each company's recruiting record. "In fact, Joe, I close 99% of all my recruiting presentations."

Sleaze also explained how the free world should beat a path to his door for marketing advice, economic planning, and the philosophy of success. If only his previous eight companies had listened to his advice, he'd still be with them setting bigger recruiting records. Those companies couldn't support downlines. Sleaze would sign up the distributors, but his recruits would drop out from home office apathy. That's why Sleaze had sponsored under Joe. Joe's group had few dropouts. This would be the company where Sleaze could recruit and keep an active downline.

"Hey Joe, got any leads for me to sponsor? Most of my contacts are burned out. Just get me in front of a prospect and I guarantee I'll close him." Sleaze was ready to start fast.

"I have a referral from one of my best customers," Joe replied. "Seems like this guy John and his wife, Mary, need to earn some extra money. Could be a good prospect. Are you sure you want to make the presentation? Wouldn't you want to watch how I do it first?"

"Naw. I saw your presentation when you signed me up. No offense, but it was the most lukewarm, weak, puppy dog pitch ever to nauseate the selling profession. You even forgot to press for the close! Let me show you how a real man gives a presentation."

"The Sleaze organization will make me look like a superstar," thought Distributor Joe. "His downline alone should make me a few thousand dollars a month. Talk about recruiting dynamite! This guy's motivated."

Mr. Close in action

Later that evening, Sleaze was pitching John and Mary while Joe sat back and took notes.

"You love your family, don't you? So why not join and make the extra money they need to live the type of life they deserve? You do love your family, right?" Sleaze was going in for the kill.

John squirmed a bit and said, "Well, sure I love them. I just don't see how I could successfully do this program. I don't have many contacts."

"John, it's a matter of desire. Some people have it, others are just *wimps*. You look like the type of guy who has guts. What do ya say you sign right here and get started?"

"I want some time to think it over. It's a big decision. My wife and I usually talk these kind of decisions over for a few days."

"What's the big decision?" Sleaze was really warming up now. "It only costs $50 for a kit! You spend more than that on a good pair of shoes or on a night on the town. Don't be so cheap. You're thinking small. This is a big opportunity. Sign right here and whip out that old checkbook, okay?"

"Hey, I'm not cheap. I just want a little time to make the right decision. Surely this opportunity will be here tomorrow, won't it?"

John stared at the paper but didn't move. Sleaze decided it was time to force the action.

"Opportunities won't wait for losers. There are two types of people in life, the decision makers and the losers. Don't you think it's time you change, make a commitment, and do something worthwhile with your life? So what size of starter inventory you want? The $100 starter pack or the $500 leader pack?"

John replied, "I'm sorry, I'm just not sold on the product. It's too expensive to retail to the people I know."

"John, when Ben Franklin had a tough decision to make, he'd write down on a piece of paper all the reasons for going ahead and all the reasons why not. Whichever side had the most reasons determined his decision. Tell your kids to go get a blank sheet of paper so we can wrap this thing up."

John's defenses began to crumble. "Sleaze, what's the minimum price to get started?"

"Fifty bucks."

"Fine, here's a check for $50. Let me read over the manuals and I'll call you next week when I'm done."

With a big smile, Sleaze gave John a pen. "John, you just hold the pen still while I jiggle the application and we'll get you signed up."

On the way back from their two-on-one presentation, Sleaze instructed Distributor Joe. "The tough battles are the most satisfying. John and Mary didn't put up much of a struggle compared to some of my other great presentations. Still, I'm sure it gave you a good example of the benefits of having a good close."

Distributor Joe nodded. "I have to admit I would never have closed John and Mary. Guess I've been too soft in the past. I have missed a lot of downline bonuses by letting presentations slip away. Maybe I should take a few closing lessons from you. I sure would like to close 100% of my presentations like you do."

"If closers make the big bucks in sales, I guess the same could hold true in MLM. Sleaze, I'll set a bunch of appointments this week for two-on-ones. We are going to be a great one-two punch."

Closing The Hard Ones

Sleaze and Joe breezed through the week. Prospects were defenseless against the high-powered closes of Sleaze. No objection was too difficult. No prospect excuses were accepted. Joe thought, "Where was Sleaze when I started? I could be retired by now. We would have signed up everyone in the state."

Their hardest close was Joe's attorney. She was a barracuda who enjoyed humiliating salesmen before chopping them into minnow bait. With Sleaze at his side, all things were possible. Joe set the appointment with the attitude, "What do I have to lose? It's Sleaze versus a professional dream killer. I'll just stand by and watch the carnage."

The first blow came from the legal expert. "Sleaze, this looks like a pyramid you have Joe into. As his attorney, I must advise him to stay away from unscrupulous hustlers like you. Has the District Attorney investigated this?"

This was merely small armsfire to Sleaze. "Ma'am, I have a lot of uneducated people that see this program. That's usually their first impression. Closer observation by intelligent, professional people, like yourself, reveals that multilevel marketing is a unique, ethical way of bypassing the middleman. Companies then pass on the savings to the consumer. It's an ingenious way of doing business, don't you think?"

"That's easy for you to say, Sleaze, but I can't go around hustling my professional colleagues to sell products. I'd be the laughing stock of my country club."

"Ma'am, false pride is a sign of an inferiority complex. You got to start thinking more of yourself. Your personal financial earnings are more important than any of your social contacts. Let your hair down; don't be such a snob."

Joe's attorney started to open up. "Sleaze, why don't you go back to the used car lot where you belong? I will not have my intelligence insulted by something that slithered out from under a rock. I'm not interested – PERIOD."

"Little Lady, I felt the same way when I first saw this program. Finding out I was financially deficient, and didn't have the backbone to do something about it, really struck a nerve. The first thing I did was get mad, just like you. But as one professional to another, we really shouldn't let our emotions taint the facts. We need to make good, solid, business decisions without reverting to childish tantrums. You agree that we should stay with the facts, don't you?"

"The facts are, Sleaze, that while your products may be good, you personally, are disgusting."

"Listen Sweets, I'm willing to take your verbal abuse if it helps you make the right decision. My only goal is to help people break through their self-imposed barriers to join the wonderful world of multilevel marketing. If I upset your delicate psyche along the way, I'm willing to take the blame. I just want what's right for you. You did say the products were good, didn't you?"

"I have no complaint about the quality of the products." Joe's attorney was mellowing.

"Fine," Sleaze replied. "If you like the products, don't you think it makes more sense to buy them at wholesale than at retail? So why not become a distributor and enjoy our wholesale purchasing privileges? Surely that makes sense."

"I have a court case in five minutes. See my secretary on the way out. She'll give you a check for a kit. My time is too valuable to spend here. Joe, next time you visit ... come alone."

On the way down the elevator, Joe was in a daze. Sleaze had just closed his most unlikely prospect and hardly worked up a sweat. Did Sleaze always feel superior at every presentation? It was obvious Sleaze thought little of his competition. Leaving the elevator, Sleaze simply remarked, "She must have passed the bar on looks."

New distributor follow-up

The monthly training meeting was the focus of Distributor Joe's organization. Throughout the month, leaders and distributors worked on two-on-one presentations for recruiting and retailing. This group meeting was the chance to get recharged. While it was officially called a training meeting, Big Al had taught Joe how to make the meeting the launching pad for next month's business. The meeting had four goals:

1. Welcome new distributors to the positive group dynamics of Joe's organization.

Most new distributors felt alone for the first few days or weeks in their career. It usually was just their sponsoring leaders and themselves going from one presentation to another. Here was a chance to see themselves as part of a bigger group. Identifying with fellow distributors created a common bond, a camaraderie, that would help sustain their enthusiasm for the business when times got tough.

2. A time to set goals.

Distributors would compare their monthly production in conversation and be inspired to set higher personal quotas out of a sense of competition. If a distributor had a slow month, his belief in the program could be rekindled by hearing of another's success.

3. Sell product.

Joe would have several distributors give personal testimonials and relate product success stories from their customers. New distributors would order many of the products to realize the same benefits.

4. Training.

A guest speaker, such as Big Al, would share his techniques for building successful organizations. Improving the downline's skill helped improve its attitude. Everyone was anxious to leave the training meetings and try out the newest techniques. The training speaker was always the last on the program. It was important to send the group out on a positive note.

Joe felt that tomorrow night's training meeting would be the best ever. New distributors always brought enthusiasm to the group. Since Sleaze and Joe had recruited 25 new people in the last two weeks, this meeting would sizzle. Joe could introduce his newest star, Sleaze Shallowman, and announce to his group that Sleaze would be the featured speaker at the following month's training meeting. The distributors would hardly be able to hold back their excitement knowing that Joe's superstar would be sharing his wisdom at the next training meeting.

But first, the reminder phone calls had to be done. Every month Joe called each distributor in his downline to remind him of the meeting. It was a chance to sell the distributor on the importance of attending, and boosted attendance.

Joe called John and Mary first. "Hi, John. It's Joe. Haven't heard from you since Sleaze and I were at your house two weeks ago. Had a chance to read the manual? Do you remember that tomorrow night is our big group meeting?"

John replied, "Sorry, Joe. Can't make it. Tomorrow night I have to brush the dog. You know how it is. Got to take care of things."

"Uh, John, uh, are you sure you can't make it?" Joe was a bit flustered.

"Sorry, Joe. Have to run. Make sure to give me a call next month. Bye."

Joe hung up the phone and thought, "No big deal. There's twenty four new recruits to call. One no-show won't even be noticed."

Joe's lawyer couldn't make it either. "Got to roll up the garden hose tomorrow night. Never know when someone will trip and sue. Can't be too careful these days. Liability insurance premiums are on the rise. Give me a call next month, Joe."

Twenty three more phone calls brought twenty three more excuses.

"Need to wax my bowling ball tomorrow."—"My mother's neighbor's sister's aunt is ill. We'll be visiting her." —"I think my in-laws are coming to supper tomorrow."—"That's a work night."—"That's my day off."—"That's family night. The family goes out to the movies while I sit home and drink beer." And so the list continued.

Joe sank into a mini-depression. "I've never had this happen before. I'd better call Sleaze. He'll know what to do." The last two weeks with Sleaze had been a mind-expanding trip. Surely, Joe's newest hero, Sleaze, could give him the magic words to persuade the new distributors to come to the meeting. This really was strange.

Grabbing the phone, Joe dialed the answerman. "Hey Sleaze, I have a problem. I just called all our new recruits and no one is coming to tomorrow night's meeting. Help!"

"Joe, you can't expect to have my great closing skills by watching me for only two weeks. I'm a trained professional. I know how to corner the prospect's emotions and leave the beaten prospect with only one way out – my way. So don't feel bad that you can't instantly duplicate my success. Greatness doesn't come easy."

"That's easy for you to say, Sleaze, but what do I do about tomorrow night's meeting?"

"Joe, don't worry about those no-show cry babies. If they don't want to work, we'll get new ones. There's a pigeon at every house. Set a few more appointments and we'll hit the street again. We make a great team. Let's not spoil our organization with a bunch of proven notworkers."

After hanging up the phone, Joe didn't feel any better. It was time to call Big Al. Maybe he would have a suggestion. A meeting without the new recruits didn't seem right.

The real problem

"Come over to my house and we'll make a few phone calls," said Big Al. "It won't take long to get to the bottom of this mystery."

Distributor Joe couldn't wait to get to Big Al's house. The meeting was tomorrow night, so there was little time to waste.

Joe listened to Big Al's first phone call to John and Mary.

"Sorry, Big Al, we really have to brush the dog. No way we can make it to tomorrow night's meeting. I haven't even reviewed the sales manual I bought when Joe and Sleaze were here."

"Are you sure this business is what you really want to do?" asked Big Al. "Sounds like you are pretty busy now and won't be able to put in the time necessary to make your business grow. Are you sure you made the right decision to become a distributor?"

John was quiet. Finally, he said, "Well, you are right. I really didn't want to become a distributor. It's just that it was worth $50 to get Sleaze out of our house. We don't have the time or the interest in distributing products.

Maybe you can buy our kit back or give it to someone who needs it. Tell Joe we like him a lot, but the business isn't for us."

After Big Al hung up, he turned to Joe and said, "What do you think of John's answer? I took the pressure off and he admitted the business wasn't for him."

Joe said, "I think I'm getting the picture. Let's call my lawyer."

Joe's lawyer confirmed Joe's suspicions. "My time is worth $125 an hour. It was worth the $50 to get Sleaze out of my office. He could argue all day. I had more important appointments and projects than listening to that peddler."

The rest of Big Al's and Joe's phone calls to new distributors were identical. They admitted to being high-pressured or embarrassed into joining Joe's company. Some admitted that they couldn't visualize themselves as high-pressure closers like Sleaze. If they had to be obnoxious like Sleaze to succeed, they didn't want any part of the business.

"Sounds like you and Sleaze burned off a bunch of good prospects, Joe. You see, multilevel marketing is an all-volunteer business. If we high-pressure our prospects, will they continue to volunteer? Probably not. Plus, people don't like high-pressure closers. They won't welcome them back into their homes again and try to avoid further contact with them at meetings. Since multilevel marketing is built on long-term relationships, maybe you should go back to using the *Million Dollar Close*."

Multilevel marketing is built on long-term relationships. Would your prospects want a long-term relationship with Sleaze Shallowman?

The million dollar close

Want a sure fire close that puts motivated, self-starters into your group? Want a close that is not high-pressure? Want a close that has built solid, successful organizations? Then you will want to use the Million Dollar Close!

Here is how it works. When you finish your presentation, look at your prospect and say:

"Well, what do you think?"

That's it. Nothing more. Just sit and listen.

Your prospect will now have to make a decision. You have presented the facts, so now it is up to the prospect to decide if the business is for him. If your prospect says: "Sounds pretty good." – you give him an application and sponsor him into your company. Your prospect has now made his own decision without artificial pressure from you. He wants to do it.

If your prospect says:

"I don't know. I'm pretty busy. Most of my friends wouldn't like this. The products are too expensive. Do you have a copy of the president's 1974 income tax return? I don't want to go to meetings, etc." – don't sponsor him.

You have enough grief and babysitting with your present distributors, so why ask for more? The prospect has made a decision not to join. Respect his right to run his life as he sees fit. Not everyone must think exactly as you do.

So why do we call this the Million Dollar Close? Because distributors who use it – make money. The prospects they sponsor want to do the business. They come to meetings. They set appointments. They want training. You don't have to beg and cajole these distributors. They are self- motivated.

What if you didn't use the Million Dollar Close? What if you spent the next two hours answering every objection? What if you promised to remove every obstacle for your prospect? What would you have? A weak distributor that would blame you for his lack of progress. You would spend valuable months of your career inviting this prospect to meetings he wouldn't attend, to trainings he wouldn't attend, to two-on-ones he couldn't make, etc. If you were really dedicated, you could go into group counseling with this unmotivated distributor for the next five years so you could change his thinking to be your thinking.

Can you afford a five-year investment in an unmotivated prospect?

So, what do the smart distributors who use the Million Dollar Close do with the prospects who don't join? They give their names and phone numbers to their competition. This keeps the competition busy while the smart distributors go out and find the good prospects.

For your consideration:

1. By using the Million Dollar Close, "Well, what do you think?", are we sorting versus convincing?

2. Will your prospects appreciate the opportunity to make their own decision?

3. How much time do you waste with marginal distributors who constantly complain?

4. Wouldn't it be fun to work only with self-motivated distributors?

5. How good are distributors that insist on extra benefits and freebies before they'll join your company?

6. Would you feel more comfortable just explaining the opportunity and then letting the prospect decide?

Building trust

A distributor passed away and went to heaven. Arriving at the pearly gates, St. Peter said, "Come on in. I'll show you around. You'll like it here."

Walking through the gates, the distributor noticed clocks everywhere. There were grandfather clocks, wall clocks, watches, and clocks in every corner. It appeared that heaven was nothing more than a giant clock warehouse.

Surprised at how heaven looked, the distributor asked, "St. Peter, what's the deal? Why are all these clocks here in heaven?"

St. Peter replied, "The clocks keep track of things on earth. There is one clock for each person. Every time the person on earth tells a lie, his clock moves one minute."

"For instance, this clock is for Sam, the used car salesman. If you watch it closely, it will move."

"Click." The minute hand on Sam's clock moved one minute. "Click." It moved another minute. "Sam must be into closing a customer right now," said St. Peter. "The minute hand on his clock moves all day."

The distributor and St. Peter continued walking. Soon, they came to a clock with cobwebs on the minute hand. "Whose clock is this?" asked the distributor.

"That clock belongs to the Widow Mary. She is one of the finest, God-fearing, people on earth. I bet her clock hasn't moved in a year or two."

They continued walking and touring heaven. The distributor enjoyed watching the clocks of all his friends. When the tour was finished, the distributor said, "I've seen everyone's clock but Sleaze Shallowman's. Where is his clock?"

Saint Peter smiled, "Just look up. We use his clock for a ceiling fan."

How do your customers, prospects, and distributors perceive your credibility? Are you known as an honest, straight- shooter? Or, are you considered a salesman who exaggerates facts to make a sale?

Successful multilevel leaders build trust into their relationships. They undersell, not oversell. Unlike direct sales where a relationship may only last for one presentation, multilevelers work side by side for a career. You can't stretch the truth today and hope your distributors and customers will trust you tomorrow. Long-term multilevel income comes from long-term distributors and customers.

Here are a few examples to illustrate the difference between underselling and overselling:

#1. Vitamins

Worst: These vitamins cure arthritis and are suppressed by a secret conspiracy of the American Medical Association. They fear that if the public knows, they'll all be put out of business.

Real bad: These vitamins cure arthritis.

Bad: These vitamins usually cure arthritis. You'll see the difference in less than a week.

Better: Many people with arthritis swear by these vitamins because it cured their arthritis.

Best: People with arthritis should at least try these vitamins. The body can do wonders if properly nourished. What do you have to lose?

#2. Opportunity

Worst: You are going to be rich. Just pull out your checkbook and let's get started.

Real bad: This is the greatest opportunity of the twentieth century. To pass this by would be throwing your entire life and future away.

Bad: Never in the history of mankind has such an opportunity occurred.

Better: There is no better opportunity available today.

Best: This opportunity is the break you have been waiting for. Why not take advantage of it?

See the difference? Prospects buy from people they trust.

For your consideration:

1. How can I make my meetings and personal presentations more believable?

2. Can I build credibility by underselling a product and overproving in the product demonstration?

3. What characteristics make my upline leaders believable?

4. How do prospects feel when they discover the opportunity or product is even better then originally presented?

The presentation ratings game

Most games are fun. This game can make you rich.

You'll need a pencil and a desire to play fair. Your honest answers to this test are important. Then you can compare what the prospect wants versus what you deliver.

Professional salesmanship is delivering what the prospect wants to buy. Therefore, we should look at the recruiting presentation through the prospect's eyes.

A survey of multilevel prospects asked what they wanted in a recruiting presentation. Ten factors were presented, and the prospects were asked to rate them in order of importance.

Here is your chance to pretend you are a prospect. Please rate the following ten factors in order of importance for making a decision to join a multilevel company. Place the number (1) next to the most motivating factor, the number (2) next to the second most motivating factor, etc. When you have numbered the factors in order of importance from 1 to 10, turn the page to see how the prospects rated the factors.

Make sure you fill out the test before you turn the page. Cheating will result in automatic qualification for the Sleaze Shallowman Ethics Award.

Ten Factor Rating Game

___ Company literature shown

___ Marketing plan and potential earnings

___ Training provided

___ Who gave the presentation

___ Product line

___ Company management experience

___ Upline support

___ Company image

___ Sales kit provided

___ Being first in area

"The Egyptian Attorney General hereby orders your arrest for building an illegal pyramid."

How the prospects rated the factors

#1 *Who gave the presentation*

This won by a landslide. The #1 reason a prospect joins a multilevel company is YOU. The prospect can't see or touch the company. The prospect does not have personal experience with the product line. The prospect has not visited with the home office. All the prospect sees is YOU.

What about literature? Or videos? Consider this. If John Wayne presents a multilevel opportunity on the back of a matchbook cover, you'd still be impressed. However, if a drunken vagrant showed you a video, would you join? The prospect is looking at YOU.

Your prospect will be working with you – not with videos, flip charts, or the national marketing director. His thoughts throughout your presentation are:

"Can I work effectively with you?" "Will you take the time to help me?" "Can you do the job?" "Are you telling the truth?" "Will you turn off my contacts?" "Can I trust you?" "Are you committed, or just a peddler?" "Are you giving me a memorized pitch, or really talking to me?" "Will you have the patience to train me while I learn?" "Do you only want my application and money?" "Do you believe in me?"

How the prospect perceives you is the most important factor in his decision to join. Doesn't it make sense to improve your presentation image?

As a bad example of this concept, consider the following scenario. The motivated distributor spends the presentation hammering home memorized facts such as:

A. Where the president and founder was born. Come on. Does it really matter which county in Southern Montana was his place of birth?

B. The 49 incredible uses of Super-Duper Cleaner. Wouldn't one or two uses be sufficient? Of course. Does the prospect really need to know the molecular co-efficient of the viscosity inherent to surfactants exposed to non-petroleum surfaces at less than 4.57 degrees Centigrade? (And don't forget to read the laboratory report in full.)

C. What type of car your upline qualified for under the 9 Star PV/BV/CV regional leaders conference qualification. Does your prospect care what kind of car someone else is driving? Or, does he care if you can help him achieve the car of his dreams?

D. A forty-five minute presentation on the marketing plan. Does 7% on level two mean anything in real terms to a prospect? Is 7% better than 6.5%? He isn't even sure about the product acceptance of his friends and neighbors. Sure, we can get excited about the brand new achiever bonus added by the company last week. But does the prospect have a basis to appreciate the finer points of the distributor compensation package?

It's clear that the presentation facts are less important than the prospect's perception of YOU.

#2 Upline support

This translates into YOU again. The second most important factor rated by multilevel prospects was their ability to depend on their upline (YOU and others) to help them become successful. In every presentation the products are wonderful and the compensation is wonderful. Yet, many prospects won't join. The reason? They don't believe they can do it.

Your prospect may be new to multilevel marketing. He will be unsure of his ability to translate his present skills into multilevel skills. In fact, your prospect may not even have the faintest idea on how to start. His future is in your hands.

What's more important than upline support to his career? Not much. Soothe your prospect's insecurities by showing how you and your sponsor have helped others become successful. Assure your prospect of upline support until he has reached a certain self-sufficient level of success. Your prospect wants to be successful. You hold the key. Why not stress your commitment to his long-term development?

Some phrases that should not be part of your presentation are:

"I think this company is going to do well." "Of course, I am also a distributor for several other companies." "If you don't like this program, I've got some more to show you." "If this doesn't work for us, I know another company we can try."

#3 Training provided

Does your group have weekly or monthly training meetings? Seminars? Rallies? This is the classroom training your prospect will be looking for. And that's only half the story.

"On-the-job" training is what really sells your prospect. Why did franchises take off in the 70's and 80's? They offered a company-trained mentor to work at the franchisee's location to help them off to a fast start. The purchaser of the franchise felt secure with the addition of the on-the-job training.

Help solve your prospect's fear of the unknown by emphasizing your own personal on-the-job training, the two-on-one presentations. Tell your prospect you will give the recruiting presentations to his prospects while he observes. Anyone can feel confident if all they have to do is observe. Once your prospect feels he has sufficient skills and group-building success, then he may decide to continue without your help.

Prospects like to buy "sure things." Make his success a sure thing with your commitment for continuing on-the-job training.

#4 Marketing plan and earnings potential

Surprised? The money doesn't show up as a factor in the prospect's decision process until #4. Promises of earnings are meaningless without the prospect's confidence that he can work the business successfully. Or, in other words, who cares if you earn 99% commission if you are selling ice to Eskimos?

The belief that the prospect can succeed in the business transcends the percentages in the marketing plan.

Remember your first exposure to multilevel marketing? Could you go home and completely explain the finer points of the compensation plan after only one exposure? Probably not. So don't spend too much time making a big deal out of the 1/2 of 1% super override bonus on non-qualifying directors on a regional basis. It won't help your prospect make a decision to join.

Recruiting professionals concentrate on a few basic points in the compensation plan, explaining it in layman's terms.

Some parts of the compensation plan explanation that can be saved for training are:

"Non-encumbered volume", "PV as related to distributor net", "Freight adjustment factors", "Roll up commissions", "Group quota differentials", "Grand Puba titles".

#5 Product line

A good way to irritate prospects is to demonstrate every product in detail. An eager prospect wants to know one thing about the product line: Will people buy it? Your product may have gold plated bearings instead of stainless steel bearings. So what? If no one will buy your product, does it matter how wonderful the quality is?

Your prospect does not want to join a company with products people don't want. Professional recruiters concentrate on showing the market for their products and why the general public desires to have the product. You can handle product quality and credibility with a few short demonstrations, testimonials, or support material such as laboratory reports.

#6 Being first in area

Maybe he's not the pioneer to blaze the trail, but your prospect wants to see a large potential of qualified prospects. Assure your prospect that together, you can actively create a viable business. This is already a very minor point as we are in the bottom half of decision factors for the prospect.

#7 Company literature shown

Beautiful literature doesn't sell; people sell. If you are relying on 70 lbs. four-color enameled stock with artistic photographs to sign up prospects, maybe you should reconsider your career and become a photographer. If you are a jerk passing out nice-looking flyers, you are still a jerk. Do you think your prospect wants to bring a jerk to do a two-on-one presentation with his friends, neighbors, and relatives? Ha! Ha! Ha! Well, jerks think so anyway.

#8 Company image

You are making a presentation to your best prospect in Miami, Florida. You show him a beautiful video describing the 45,000 square foot home office on 3 acres in the exclusive suburb of Olympia Fields, in the town of Flossmoor, Illinois. Big deal. So what if the company has a lot of money for videos, offices, printing, etc.? The real question is: "Can my potential sponsor do the job? Will he be capable of helping me reach the success I desire?"

After all, what can the home office really do to help? Send the prospect another video? Oh, wow, that will surely help to build his business.

#9 Sales kit provided

A fine collection of reading material, brochures, sales receipts, videos, cassettes, etc.; all totally worthless in the hands of a prospect lacking confidence. Prospects get confidence and support from their upline, not from ballpoint pens and bumper stickers with the company logo.

Inside joke of multilevel pros: "Here's your kit. Go for it."

#10 Company management experience

"Our president had 2.173 years of public auditing experience with one of the largest regional firms in the South Atlantic States. His grading on his personnel report by his superiors was 2.46, one of the highest ever given." Pretty ludicrous, isn't it?

What not to say:

"Our president has 12 years experience in multilevel management with 8 different companies."

For your consideration:

Well, how did you do? Did your answers match what our prospect survey showed?

Is your presentation giving prospects what they want to buy? Or, is your presentation giving your prospects what's important to you?

What parts of your current presentation need to be emphasized? Do you disagree with the prospects' answers to the survey?

Maybe in your opinion the prospects should have rated the factors differently. What's more important? How the prospects look at your presentation or how you think they should look at it?

What are you going to do different?

Do you promise not to laugh during someone else's presentation when they explain the molecular co-efficient of the viscosity inherent to surfactants exposed to non- petroleum surfaces at less than 4.57 degrees Centigrade?

Handicapped by money

Do you need money to make money in multilevel? Only if you want to start with a handicap.

A few years ago, a prosperous banker discovered the potential of multilevel marketing. What a concept! Here were a few blue collar, "mom & pop" distributors making big money with no business experience. Some of his "illiterate" customers were making two and three times as much money as his vice-presidents with their MBAs. These amateur business people had no marketing or business plan. They didn't know a P & L from a P/E ratio. They even considered their work ... fun!

"Just think what I could do with this multilevel business with my vast business experience," thought the banker. "I have about $75,000 I can use as seed money to get my business up and going. Should be enough to bury my amateur competition."

The best way to get exposure is to advertise. The banker bought the back page of a prominent trade journal for four months and received 600 leads. There were too many people to call personally, so the banker sent them a letter and an expensive evaluation pack. Total cost? $18,000 for this campaign. Results? A few multilevel junkies joined who wanted the banker to buy some downliners for their organizations.

"Total waste of advertising dollars," said the banker. "Insufficient follow-up blew my campaign. Ordinary business people would have read my literature and made a decision to join. I guess these folks just can't read."

Next, the banker bought an even more expensive advertising campaign. This time he hired full-time employees to handle the follow-up. Their job was to call and, if necessary, fly to the prospects and sign them into the program.

The results? His employees were just that: employees. A jobholder never has the same motivation level as a business owner. The prospects looked at the employees and said, "If the opportunity is so good, why are you an employee?" The prospects wanted to join an opportunity where the presenter believed in the opportunity too. Total cost? $50,000.

The banker invested the remaining $7,000 in a company-sponsored warehouse program. He turned the location into a retail store operation and quickly lost his remaining investment.

You can't buy multilevel success. You must earn it the old-fashioned way: **work**. Give a new distributor a lot of money to invest in his business and you succeed in delaying his progress.

Do you need money to succeed in multilevel marketing? Only if you want to start with a handicap.

The swap

"I need to get new blood into my local organization." Distributor Joe wanted some fast results. "If I recruit and train multilevel amateurs, it will take a long time before they produce the big volumes. I need volume now. I wonder where I could get a source of trained, experienced multilevel distributors?"

Sound familiar? Doesn't everyone want the secret shortcut to instant volume? Here is how to do it.

Take a look at your organization. Do you have a few dropouts, burnouts, and quitters? Everyone has turnover in his multilevel group. We try to minimize turnover, but it will always be with us.

Why did some of your downline quit? Of course it is never our fault, so here are a few reasons distributors leave our organizations:

1. They have lost the dream. When they left the original opportunity meeting, there were stars in their eyes and visions of multilevel wealth. Success didn't come instantly so they lost their motivation. No motivation – no work. No work – no success.

2. They have personality conflicts with their uplines. It happens all the time. The world doesn't guarantee harmony. They dropped out because their uplines didn't help them enough, didn't appreciate them, talked badly behind their backs, insulted their spouses, took advantage of their efforts, etc. "I'm certainly not going to work this business and enrich my stupid sponsor!" So, they quit.

3. They have bad chemistry with their uplines. They are Democrats; their uplines are Republican. They enjoy big production meetings; their uplines like quiet two-on-ones. They never smile; their uplines like to party. It's not much fun working with someone you have little in common with.

4. They were not compatible with the products. Some distributors like high-repeat, consumable, low-price items. Others enjoy the challenge of high-ticket sales presentations. Heavy smokers and drinkers get tired of going to health-nut meetings where they receive constant lecturing.

5. The colors on the company letterhead are wrong. Hey, any excuse will do.

6. Some quitters just don't like you. Admittedly, this is extremely rare. However, there have been one or two instances in the history of multilevel.

Now, ask yourself, "How many of my quitters can I get back into my group?"

Your answer should be: "Few or none."

When distributors leave, it is similar to a divorce. Even if the married couple gets back together, it's never really the same the second time around. Re-sponsored distributors don't have the same wide-eyed enthusiasm and motivation as they do the first time around. The dream is dead. Now it's just business.

So let's say you have 20 former distributors in your file. They have no value to you, but would they to someone else?

Absolutely! You have an asset of 20 trained, experienced distributors who are looking for different circumstances.

Do you think you are the only one in the world with distributor turnover?

Your competitor across town would love to have your rejects. Your ex-distributors may never want to work with you again, but your competitor could be their guiding light to success.

Why not trade your 20 ex-distributor leads for 20 ex-distributor leads from your competitor?

You can't lose (you already lost your quitters). You have everything to gain from 20 fresh leads of trained, experienced distributors.

Will your competitor trade? Sure. It's the classic "win-win" situation. He gets to unload his non-producers for new prospects. He is going to love it.

What about the ex-distributors? They win too. Fresh leadership, better chemistry, new dreams, and better corporate colors on the stationery add up to a fresh start for success.

But don't stop with just multilevel marketing leads. You can swap leads with non-multilevel salespeople. Why not swap leads with insurance brokers or automobile sales managers? The possibilities are endless.

You can even swap items in your product line for leads.

Multilevel junkies

Junkie – a schizophrenic MLM distributor who believes that belonging to several companies will multiply his income proportionately. A person addicted to spending money on sign-up kits.

How junkies think.

If one MLM program is good, then two programs should be twice as good! Three programs would be even better. Hey, what about four programs? That's it, I'll join *seven* different programs. Now I'll have one program for every day of the week.

I'll do *program #1* on Sundays. All the new prospects I meet on Sunday should join *program #1*. Of course if the prospect is more suited to *program #4's* product line, then I'll sign my new Sunday prospect into Thursday's *program #4*. That would mean I should reciprocate by spending some time on Thursday's *program #4* cross-promoting into Sunday's *program #1* to make up the difference.

But then again, if my Sunday prospect in *program #4* were to come across a prospect that would be more suited for *program #6,* which I work on Tuesdays, well, I would have to sign up my Sunday *program #4's* prospect in the *Tuesday program #6* so he could sign up his new prospect.

If my Sunday prospect is to duplicate my efforts, then he'll have to sign up in all seven programs. If all seven programs don't suit him, maybe he should sign up into 10 or 12 different programs that suit him better.

What if I have a second level distributor in *program #47* who wants to sponsor his upline into a different program? Or, what if my group grows and we find out we are promoting 87 different programs? Our meetings could consist of recruiting each other into different uplines, downlines, crosslines, etc. Maybe we should have a lottery to settle this whole thing.

MLM is a business of *duplication*. It is just that simple. Successful leaders concentrate on building a few good leaders, and making them successful. That is hard work, even in just one program!

How good a mind reader are you? Are you able to look at a prospect and instantly determine whether he is better suited for Wednesday's *program #66* or Thursday's *program #53*? Or, must you show your prospect all 70 programs, confuse him, and get nowhere?

"Don't like this one? Wait, let me show you five more programs."

What will the prospect think if you are not personally focused?

Speaking of duplication, if you have trouble mind-reading, don't you think your new distributors will have even more trouble?

Let's face facts. Junkies haven't thought out the reality of their business. For instance, which makes more sense?

1. Work seven programs, but only put forth 1/7 of your time and effort in each. Wouldn't that mean you would only receive 1/7 of the possible income in each program?

2. Work one program and put 100 percent of your effort towards success?

Seems pretty clear, doesn't it? Successful millionaires know the surest path to success is to have *one focused goal.* You can't go seven different directions simultaneously. It is like having a job at a different company every day of the week. Chances are you won't make it to the top in any of those companies. Have you ever heard of "President for a day"?

More trouble.

How can a junkie justify going to his distributor and say: "Today's new program is better than the program I introduced to you yesterday. And it is much better than the program I introduced to you three days ago. Remember the program we joined last week when I said it was the best ever? Well , this new program is the newest best ever." The junkie loses so much face introducing new programs that weekly face lifts are needed.

Seriously, how many distributors will want to follow a leader who doesn't know where he is going? The world is full of people searching for leaders to follow. That's why focused, single-company MLM leaders have an easier time sponsoring. Maybe it is easier for focused leaders because the competition is so scarce.

Today's junkies have formed a cult of their own. With the emergence of networking, each junkie has the names and addresses of several hundred or thousand fellow junkies. When a new program comes out, your ordinary junkie now becomes **SUPER JUNKIE.** Super junkie differs from an ordinary junkie because super junkies come equipped with a stamp-licking option. Every new program will have the junkie cult sending recruiting letters to each other. And every letter will say the same thing:

"Get in now. Be first. Sign up under me. I am close to the top. This is the real winner. It's better than the last 16 real winners I sent you. If you get in now, you can mail to other junkies first."

And so the mailings go. If you are unlucky enough to be on the junkie mailing lists, you could receive 20 or more identical offers within a week. Only a few people can be first, so the rest of the junkies soon quit. Now they can be first in the next new program and sponsor their previous uplines to be their downlines. And so the cycle continues, junkies sponsoring junkies who re-sponsor junkies who... well, you get the idea.

No one ever makes any real money. How could they? A junkie is only in a program for a month or two. If they stayed any longer, they couldn't be first in the next program.

71

Then who makes the money?

The U.S. Post Office! Every new program means an increase in stamp revenue. Some knowledgeable MLM leaders suspect that most new MLM programs are started by the U.S. Post Office as a way to increase revenues.

Who are the losers?

Who really loses money from the MLM junkie cult? The junkies do, of course, but also the MLM leaders that had the junkies infiltrate their groups! Nothing can contaminate, poison, and kill a group faster than unscrupulous junkies dividing distributors' efforts into cross-sponsoring upline, downline, crossline, etc. Once a junkie gets a name in your downline, your downline distributor will receive junkie trash mail until the day he moves and leaves no forwarding address.

Is there a cure? We can't say. At present, no MLM junkie detoxification center exists. Rehabilitation through counseling hasn't proved to be effective. But rumor has it, that soon there will be announced, a brand new MLM program offering "Junkie, Subliminal, Reprogramming Tapes". So here's your chance to sign up first! Get your upline, downline, crossline and everyone else an application quick. This could be your chance to get in first on the pre-announcement of the pre-launch of the chartered fast start below ground floor positions.

Me first! Me first!

Many new distributors become confused seeking financial success in MLM. They want the rewards of MLM success *before* they deposit the work and training to deserve them. After all, why should one pay his dues when a secret shortcut can be found?

New distributors are looking for ways to make money faster. An upline sponsor is earning more money. How is he doing it? He was in before the new distributor...*that must be the key.*

A new distributor believes his upline leader is successful because he got into the company on the ground floor. His upline leader surely couldn't have reached his success because of hard work and dedication. So it appears that his sponsor's good fortune exists because he got in first.

Nothing could be further from the truth. A distributor who comes into an MLM program on the ground floor and doesn't work surely can't expect success. Success comes from diligently building a strong downline of trained leaders. The ground floor means nothing. It's the amount of service and results produced that earns bonus checks.

The new distributor usually starts looking for an easy shortcut to success. If he believes his sponsor succeeded because he got in early, then it must logically follow that the new distributor must search and join the next new company so he can be in first.

What would be even better? If the new distributor could be first in joining the next new "Company Of The Week", he could recruit his original upline sponsor into his downline. What a deal!

Of course, if the new distributor is in the new company first, and his sponsor comes into his downline later, then the original sponsor must go out and search for the next new company to get in first so the original sponsor can re-recruit the new distributor back into his downline. Now things can really get exciting!

Is there really an advantage to getting in first? If an advantage was gained by being the first to join "New Company Of The Week #87", then Company #87 would not last. All the distributors that got in second with Company #87 would soon leave in quest for Company #88. That also means the distributors who joined Company #87 first will lose their downlines. So they too will leave to search for the next new opportunity.

A company must have equal opportunity for the first distributor as well as the last distributor to achieve long-term success.

The source of the mistaken belief about getting in first is the junkie cult. If a distributor joins a company on the ground floor and immediately recruits the transient junkie cult, then the ground floor distributor will initially have a substantial temporary downline. But the junkies only stay for a few weeks or hours. After they leave to search out the newest company of the week where they can be first, the ground floor distributor must then go about the business of building an MLM group the old-fashioned way: *service, hard work, and training. And if service, hard work, and training are required, most new distributors will quickly fold their tents and search for a "pre-ground floor" opportunity.*

The real problem is that many new distributors fall for the illusion, never realizing the truth.

What is the truth? It doesn't matter how close you are to the company, or even if you are sponsored by the company. Who or what is in your upline is immaterial. You are only paid on the production of your downline.

Have you ever heard of being paid an upline bonus or a "close to the company" bonus? Of course not. Financial success in MLM is based on your downline's success. That fact will not change whether you have one or 100 upline distributors between you and the company.

What's wrong with your opportunity?

Joe's prospect, Seymore, just shook his head.

"Joe, I know your opportunity can produce large incomes for people who work hard and take the business seriously. The products are fantastic. You even have a pretty good training program as far as I can tell. But Joe, your program is just too much work for me."

What a letdown from a perfect presentation. How could this be happening? Here was a prospect who really needed the opportunity to get ahead financially. The plan was perfect. The products were perfect. Even the training fit right in. Well, there was nothing else to lose, so might as well go for the high pressure close.

"Seymore, if you don't take advantage of this opportunity, you'll just go on being a loser for the rest of your life. Look at yourself. No savings, no job future, no plans for success. You need this opportunity, so sign up now."

Seymore just smiled. "You're wrong, Joe. I do have plans for success. Last night I wrote out *The Famous Seymore's Six-Point Plan For Success*. Want to read it?"

The Famous Seymore Six-Point Plan For Success

1. Lottery Tickets. Invest every spare dollar in high payoff lottery tickets. Someone has to win, so it might as well be me. Action step: Sit in front of the television every Thursday night for the weekly drawing. Develop several success cheers such as "Come on Baby! Hit my number!"

2. Apply for adoption by rich parents. If unsuccessful, convince present parents to purchase large amounts of life insurance. Action step: Encourage high-fat, low-fiber diet for parents. Hopefully they'll pass on soon so I can enjoy the proceeds while I'm still young.

3. Invest $1,000,000 in the stock market and hope for a ten percent return. The $100,000 income is slightly restrictive, but if I don't travel and buy beer on sale, I can survive comfortably without working. Action step: Hope someone loans me $1,000,000 interest-free.

4. Trade present wife for a rich heiress. So what if I'll be unhappy for the rest of my life; at least I won't have to work.

5. Hope prospectors discover gold, silver, or oil in my backyard. Action step: Quit renting and look for a free house with a backyard. Present backyard would only make my landlord happy.

6. Be jealous of everyone's success. Hope they fail and do everything to discourage them. Maybe if other people fail to get ahead, somehow, magically, I will get a rich windfall. Action step: Establish a "professional dream killer" attitude. Remind contacts that they are bound to fail.

What more could Joe say? There was nothing wrong with Joe's opportunity. *The problem was with Joe's prospect.* Again, Joe had forgotten Big Al's first lesson: <u>Look for desire, not need</u>. Seymore certainly needed the opportunity, but didn't have the desire.

Breaking even

Joe spent $42 on the help wanted ad in Sunday's newspaper. To avoid wading through endless conversations with unqualified job seekers, he structured the ad for only a few qualified responses.

Thirteen people called on Monday. After a brief explanation on the telephone, eight people agreed to meet Distributor Joe at the local restaurant over coffee to discuss the details of the opportunity.

Only three people kept their individual appointments with Joe on Tuesday night.

Prospect #1 listened intently to the presentation and said, "Sounds like I'm better off finding a part-time job that guarantees a salary. No thanks." Joe's total cost? $2 for coffee and tip. Sure was cheaper than renting a meeting room.

Prospect #2 said, "Sounds like a winner. Give me a couple of samples of the product to take home to my spouse. I want her to try some of the products before we go to your opportunity meeting tomorrow night." Joe's total cost? $2 for coffee and tip plus $6 for product samples and literature.

Prospect #3 loved the concept. "I want to go to tomorrow night's opportunity meeting and meet your other distributors. I'll bet their excitement rubs off on me. Don't bother picking me up. I'll be coming with my own carload of guests. I'm an action type of guy. Give me a couple of tapes and brochures to pass out to my friends." Joe's total cost? $2 for coffee and tip plus $8 for tapes and literature.

Only Prospect #2 and his wife showed up at Tuesday night's opportunity meeting. "Maybe Prospect #3 is lost," Joe thought. "Maybe he forgot that tonight is the meeting." A quick phone call to Prospect #3 produced a disconnected recording. "Better not bet the mortgage on that prospect. I should have picked him up," thought Distributor Joe.

Big Al gave the 35-minute opportunity meeting. At the end, Prospect #2 turned to Joe and said, "Sign us up. We'll give it a shot." Joe finished their paperwork quickly (they had a baby-sitter waiting). After a quick starter kit purchase, Joe's new recruits were on their way.

Later, Big Al and Joe met in the coffee shop. "I've got a new system," smiled Joe. "Let me tell you how I did it."

Big Al listened to Joe's recap of the last three days. "Interesting, Joe. How much did you spend to get your new recruits?"

"Uh, let me see. $42 for the ad and about $18 for coffee, samples and literature. Grand total was $60. Not too bad if I say so myself. Of course, they are untrained, and may or may not produce, but that's the risk you take on every new distributor."

Big Al asked, "I didn't see your old distributor Jack here tonight. What has happened to him?"

"You'll be sorry to hear it, but Jack quit last week. I guess I didn't give him enough attention. He sure liked the products. I'm not sure what I could have done to keep him excited."

"Have you sent him a newsletter lately?"

"No."

"Have you called and said how much you appreciate his meeting attendance and participation?"

"No."

"Have you offered to help find new prospects lately?"

"No."

Big Al continued, "Consider this. Jack and his wife barely made ends meet. What would have happened if you showed your appreciation by treating them to dinner at a fancy restaurant last night?"

Joe thought for a moment. "I'm sure they haven't had dinner out in a year or two. They'd probably think I was the greatest guy in the world."

"How much would dinner for two have cost you?"

"Less than $30."

"And you would still have Jack and his wife as loyal, trained, product-loving distributors, wouldn't you?"

"Yes, and at half the price of my new distributors."

Big Al finished their conversation by saying, "Well, congratulations for sponsoring your new distributors this evening. However, remember it is cheaper to invest time and money into keeping your present distributors, than to invest in new distributors."

"Remember, it is cheaper to invest time and money into keeping your present distributors, than to invest in new distributors."

Leadership Test

A group of distributors was sitting around having coffee after a disappointing opportunity meeting. While complaining about their lack of downline activity, one distributor said, "Hey, you know what the real problem is? The company doesn't pay enough commissions on retail sales. That's what causing my distributors to drop out."

"And you know what else the company should do?" added another distributor. "They should pay out 50% bonus on our first levels so all of our distributors will make money sooner!"

"The company should also lower prices on its products. That way we could get more people to buy," said another.

"Distributors should earn more in bonuses than what they spend for products. And the company should give free products to prospective customers. We should just have to handle reorders."

The conversation grew heated as the rest of the distributors joined in with their solutions.

"We need more support from the company. The home office is just a bunch of order takers."

"There should be a 60% bonus paid on second level distributors to help our downlines make more money."

"They should make our sponsors recruit our downlines."

"Our downlines should have higher purchasing requirements. Then we could make more overrides."

"The company should telephone our inactive distributors. Also, they should send them free newsletters for a year, in case they might get interested again."

"The real problem is that the brochures aren't wide enough. My sponsor would give me free brochures if they were wider."

"Everyone should receive a monthly bonus check, even if they don't order. Then we would have real motivation in our groups. Buying products shouldn't be mandatory."

"My dropouts would decrease if the company paid 70% bonus on the third level. And why should I spend money calling my downline? They can call me if they have problems."

"The rules should be different for me; I'm a leader."

Finally, one distributor stood up. "It seems to me we're just trying to find a way not to work. If the company and our upline did all the recruiting, selling, and motivating, why would they need us? Let's face the truth. We are paid for producing results, not for finding ways for others to earn our money. Hey, if it was easy, everyone would be a leader."

After a stunned silence, one distributor said, "Whoa, it's getting late. I'm going to miss the sports report on the evening news. See you guys next week."

Another distributor said, "I got to go to work early tomorrow. Time for me to be moving along."

The group quickly broke up and paid their checks. A few distributors made a mental note not to invite that "do-gooder" distributor to next week's coffee session.

Some people just don't understand why they get paid. They look for the free ride.

"Success is not the result of making the rules easier, but the result of overcoming obstacles."

Tale of two winners

Distributor Joe had a faithful retail base of 10 vitamin customers. Every month each customer would buy $50 of vitamins. Distributor Joe's cost was only $35, so he would make $15 on each loyal customer. The extra $150 a month was a nice addition to his monthly bonus check.

One day, after giving a recruiting presentation, the prospect stalled. "Joe, I'd like to join your MLM company, but I'm a little discouraged with direct sales. I used to sell water filters, but discovered I'm not good with cold calls or direct sales. I'm just too shy and can't face new people. I bought 20 filters from the company, but only sold filters to 10 friends. Now that they own water filters, they won't need replacements for several years. The only way to get rid of my inventory is to start cold calling. Joe, I'd rather have the IRS audit me for the last 20 years than to make a cold call."

"I don't mind servicing the 10 customers; they're my friends. It's just that they don't need another filter. I wish I was in a business like yours, selling vitamins, where there was a repeat product."

Distributor Joe said, "You have 10 customers, right? Why not join my program and sell each of your present customers $25 worth of vitamins a month? You'll make an extra $100 a month in commissions."

"Sounds great, but I'm worried about the $1,000 I've tied up in water filter inventory. Each filter cost me $100. My spouse sure won't be happy if I start a new venture with $1,000 in dead inventory sitting in our garage."

Distributor Joe said, "I have a solution that will make both of us winners. I'll trade you $1000 in vitamins for your $1,000 in water filters. The $1000 in vitamins retails for $1500. You will make $500 profit retailing them to your present 10 customers. Your friends believe in pure water, so they'll love the health benefits the vitamins provide."

Joe's prospect beamed. "Great! I'll simply supply my friends with vitamins for the next several months. I'll never have to cold call again. The best part is that I'll have my water filter investment back ($1,000) plus an extra $500 in profit. What a relief to have those water filters out of my garage! The way I see it, in a few months I'll have $1,500 in my bank account. That's sure a lot better than dead inventory in the garage. Oh yes, your new business opportunity sounds good too."

"Joe, count me in. Where do I sign?"

Closing presentations are easy when you can solve other people's problems.

After filling out the paperwork, Joe's prospect asked, "How are you going to make out, Joe? You are spending an extra $1,000 to buy vitamins for me and ending up with my old inventory. Are you sure you know what you're doing?"

Joe smiled. "My 10 good vitamin customers believe in good health and trust me. My company doesn't offer any kind of water filter, so I'm sure they'll be happy to purchase one. I'll sell each of my customers a water filter in addition to my monthly retail vitamin sales, and make an additional $1500 in sales. The extra $500 profit I'll make will be a great income boost and nice addition to my bank account. Plus, when I order the $1,000 in additional vitamins from my company, I'll qualify for a higher bonus discount. And finally, by solving your problem, I'm getting a super distributor. We'll both be winners."

Win–win situations are the trademarks of professional MLM pros.

Increasing your product volume is easy when you think of your opportunity as a *solution* to a prospect's problems.

What other excess products or services do your prospects have? Can you co-market those products or services and solve their problems?

Co-marketing can be your most effective recruiting tool.

"Increasing your product volume is easy when you think of your opportunity as a <u>solution</u> to a prospect's problems."

Why people don't join

Alex was tired of his present rut - no savings, dead-end job, credit cards charged to the limit. His family spent their yearly vacation fixing up their house, and then took an overnight camping/fishing trip to the next county. Working fifty weeks a year, a two-week vacation, and never getting ahead troubled Alex into action. He was finally ready to attend one of those "extra income opportunity meetings." His neighbor, Distributor Joe, had invited him once or twice, but never really pushed it. Joe would say, "Alex, when you're ready, let me know." Alex was ready.

When the opportunity meeting was over, Alex turned to Joe and said, "What a great meeting! What a terrific opportunity to break out of my rut! You know, I think I could really do this business with your help. I'm excited!"

"Well Alex, here's the application. If you are serious about working, you have my commitment." Joe handed Alex a pen.

"Uh, just a second Joe. I don't want to sign up tonight. I think I should at least talk it over with my wife, my accountant, and a few friends. I want to make sure I'm doing the right thing."

"Sure, Alex. No problem. Just make sure the people you talk to have your best interests at heart. Also, ask advice from someone who knows multilevel. That's the business you are entering. You wouldn't ask a plumber for legal advice, would you?"

"No, I guess not."

"Fine. Let me know what you decide. You won't be any good at this business unless you make the decision."

Later that night, Alex explained the opportunity meeting to his wife. "You had to be there. It was terrific. The best part is that we can earn 4% royalty bonus on our downline's PVs."

"What's PVs?" she asked.

"I don't really know, but it has to be important. Everybody was talking about them. Maybe it was related to supervisor's unencumbered sales. But there was a lot of money to be made with all the different types of bonuses. We can earn them with Joe's help."

Alex's wife wasn't sold. "The only bonus you ever earned was a turkey at Christmas. All you had to do to qualify was not get fired. Do you think that qualifies you for a business of your own? You can't even explain how it works! You'd better go to bed and forget this whole thing. You are getting too excited and won't be able to sleep. You have to get up early tomorrow to go to work."

Alex went to bed thinking, "Maybe I'll get another opinion tomorrow."

Alex's wife went to bed thinking, "He just wants to get rich so he can dump me for a younger woman. I didn't sacrifice 15 years of my life to get dumped now."

Breakfast was quiet at Alex's house. He left for work early to share his new dream with his fellow employees.

"Hey Frank, you gotta hear about the meeting last night. I've found a way where we both can get rich and leave this stinking job. We can work evenings after work part-time. When our bonuses are greater than our jobs here, we quit. Let me explain it, then tell me what you think. Your opinion is important to me."

While Alex attempted to explain the percentages paid on each "wonder product", Frank was thinking. "Hmmm, I've known Alex for 10 years. He's never done much before, probably won't do much in the future. He's never even taken a business course. What makes this turkey think he can start and run his own business? Besides, if we both have to work evenings, I'll miss bowling night and poker night. What about my favorite shows? Worse yet, if my wife finds out that Alex is working evenings to get ahead, she'll expect me to do it. I'd better stop this before it gets too far."

Alex finally finished his presentation. "What do you think, Frank, should we do it?"

"Naw, sounds too risky. What if we work late one night, wake up late and miss work? The boss will find out we're doing something on the side and we'll be fired. No health insurance, no dental insurance, no two weeks vacation. This selling thing might jeopardize our jobs. Sounds like a lousy idea to risk our families' financial future on a *maybe* business proposition. Let's clock in and get to work."

Alex thought, "Why am I asking Frank anything? He makes $25,000 per year. It's stupid to ask someone making $25,000 a year how to make $50,000 a year. If he knew how, he'd be doing it. I'll go visit my banker at lunch and see what he thinks."

Alex's banker listened to his story of last night's opportunity meeting. Alex was enthusiastic. "All I have to do is buy some products, sell them, and make big money. Then other people will line up at my door looking for an opportunity. I'll sign them up and make even more money."

His banker began to think. "If Alex is already one month behind on his car payment, the money he spends on products could make him fall farther behind. I'd better put a stop to this boy's foolish dreams. He doesn't need to be spending any money on an opportunity. He needs to be giving me his money."

Alex finished. "Do you think it's a good plan?"

The banker replied, "Alex, you've got it all wrong. The way to get ahead in life is to deposit money in your savings account at 6% interest. Next, you borrow money at 15% interest for a car loan. Trust me. I know about money matters. By the way, would you like to borrow some money at 23% interest to pay off your credit cards? Even though you presently pay 18% interest on the cards, we would spread out the payments so your monthly payment is less. How about a second mortgage? We have a terrific rate on them this month."

"Don't have time to talk about another loan now. I have to get back to work." Alex made a mental note to visit his lawyer after work.

Alex told his lawyer about his dream business opportunity.

While Alex talked, his lawyer thought. "I'm not even getting paid for this advice. Don't these people know I'm in this business for money? He's babbling on about marketing. I'm a lawyer. I practice law. L - A - W. I wonder if this jerk can read. If I knew about marketing, I'd be an advertising executive. I should be playing golf instead of performing a mercy mission listening to Alex. What's in it for me? If I tell him to go ahead, and it works, I won't make any money. If I tell him to go ahead, and it doesn't work, I'll look bad and still won't earn any money. I'd better tell him to drop this idea. I can still get in 9 holes."

Alex finally finished. "I trust your opinion. You've been our family's lawyer for years. Do you think I should give it a try?"

"This multilevel marketing sounds like a pyramid to me, Alex. As your trusted legal advisor, I recommend you try for overtime on your job. Besides, if you start a business, I would want to do the legal work to incorporate you, do the minutes of the corporate meetings, call in a few advisors, and charge you two or three thousand dollars. If you are going into business, you might as well do it first class. You can't afford it, Alex. Ever consider a part-time job flipping hamburgers?"

Alex was already late for dinner. His wife would be furious. Well, no harm in getting a couple more opinions before going home. She couldn't get any madder.

Alex's old classmate was a C.P.A. Why not share this income opportunity idea with him? He could find him at the local bar.

Over a few beers, Alex explained the meeting and the resistance he received from his wife, co-worker, banker, and lawyer. "So, what do you think? Is it a good idea? I want to get ahead like you."

His C.P.A. friend said, "Alex, before you enter any business opportunity, you must do several things. First, let me review your taxes. You must make business decisions with an eye towards possible tax ramifications. Second, you should hire me on retainer and expenses to investigate the company. I could fly to the home office, research the books, ask the right questions, and check the Better Business Bureau's records. Third, call my office tomorrow morning and make an appointment with my secretary. By the way, didn't you say your banker was willing to lend you money? Why not skip this business idea? I have a terrific offshore tax shelter to sell you."

Alex gulped his beer and left for home. On the way to his car he bumped into the business professor at the local college. "Say Professor, what's the secret of getting ahead financially?"

The business professor said, "Get a good job with a big company that won't lay you off. That's what I did. I have tenure. The college can't even fire me. Sure, I don't make much money, but the security is great. You'd better head home and sleep off that beer or you won't have a job tomorrow."

Alex arrived home to his wife's ultimatum. "If you show up late one more time from work, you'll be sleeping at Joe's house. Now get to bed. You've got to go to work tomorrow."

How to write a newsletter

Why should I write a newsletter for my group? I don't know how to write well. Who would type it? Printing and postage are expensive. Wouldn't it be more efficient to be out recruiting new distributors? My distributors wouldn't read it anyway.

We will look for any excuse to avoid writing newsletters, but newsletters can drastically improve your business. If you aren't writing a newsletter now, consider the following reasons why you should start writing today.

#1 Distributors love to receive them.

Most distributor mail consists of bills. It's nice to get some good news in the mail box. Your distributors want to hear what's going on in their business, especially in their local group. A little gossip sells. If you don't believe it, watch the afternoon soap operas or observe people buying trash tabloids at the supermarket checkout. Distributors want to know what's happening in their business.

#2 Increase distributor loyalty.

If you are the "phantom" sponsor, why should they work hard for you? When the next opportunity comes along, they'll leave your group. They have no reason to be loyal because you haven't earned their loyalty. At least a newsletter is an effort to support your distributor organization. It shows you care.

#3 My name in print?

When you look at a group picture, do you look for yourself first? Sure. We all want to see how we look. In a newsletter, the first thing a distributor looks for is his name. Everyone loves recognition. Many distributors will work harder for recognition than money. Here is your chance to provide the recognition the distributor doesn't receive at home or at his job. Show your appreciation and your distributors will show their loyalty.

#4 A reminder that they are in business.

Do you have distributors who only work their business sporadically? They only think about their business when you call to remind them of an upcoming meeting. Your organization may receive one newsletter a month from the home office. They look at the home office newsletter and say, "Oh yeah, we're distributors. Maybe we should buy something this month." When you send your newsletter in addition to the home office newsletter, they may purchase products twice a month.

The rewards of your organizational newsletter are worth the effort. So why do we hesitate to use this important tool to improve our business? Because we think it's hard.

Would you write a newsletter if you had a "quick write" formula?

Just follow this formula to produce your instant newsletter.

#1 Company news.

If you receive special information as a leader, this is the place to pass it on. Have you talked with the home office personnel lately? Tell a little bit about your conversation. Your distributors want to know the newest information and also any inside information you can provide. For example, you could write:

"Mary and I talked with distributor relations on Friday. They said the new product introduction of Wonder Vitamin will be announced in two weeks. Here's an inside tip. Mail your order today before the rest of the distributor force finds out about this big announcement. The home office will process orders on a first-come/first-serve basis. By having your orders in first, you'll avoid the inevitable backorder situation that will occur with a hot product like this."

#2 Recognition.

Your downline wants to see how everyone else is doing. Is Mary still the top recruiter? Who retailed the most this month? Who had the biggest party? And who had babies? Try to get as many distributor names in print as possible. If they feel their name may appear, they'll read every word of your newsletter eagerly. Some quick categories to fill up your newsletter fast are:

A. Top ten retailers.

B. Top ten recruiters.

C. Announce the name of each new distributor and the name of his/her sponsor.

D. Appreciation to distributors who helped with the last meeting.

E. Recipes from these distributors.

F. Recruiting hints from these distributors.

#3. Market product.

You earn bonuses on product movement. Use your newsletter to sell your distributors on your company's products. How? Try the following:

A. Give testimonials from your distributors and customers. Here's another chance to give recognition to your distributors.

B. If you have any lab reports or technical data, print it in your newsletter. It will sell your distributors and be a handy sales tool for retailing.

C. Suggest new uses for your present products.

D. Announce a product sale. Give 7 items for the price of six.

E. Tell how other distributors have successfully retailed certain products.

Remember, your distributors are customers, too. Your job is to encourage them to use their products. Once they are sold on a product, retailing will follow. Imply that it is un-American to buy your competitor's products.

Most distributors will never earn the big checks in multilevel, but they'll stay loyal to a product line. When your distributors love their products, your bonus checks are guaranteed.

#4 Meeting schedule.

List your upcoming opportunity meetings. Your distributors want to know the time, place, and dates. Also include training meetings and company functions. Do you have a famous upline leader coming to speak? Build it up as an important event.

#5 Type your newsletter.

Don't worry about making it fancy. Your distributors want the information, not pretty graphics. If they want to look at something nice, recommend National Geographic Magazine. They have beautiful pictures.

Trying to make your newsletter look professional hinders production. Don't worry about it. The important thing is to get it out to your organization. Just have someone type it up and head for the printer or photocopy machine.

#6 Personalize each newsletter.

You hate being a number. You hate junk mail. You love it when people remember you. Take the time to put a small handwritten note on each newsletter you mail. Your distributors will love you for caring. Will it take too much time? The real question is: Is this distributor worth a small handwritten sentence or two? The answer is "Yes!" If your downline organization is too much bother for you, why don't you consider a different career? Show your distributors you care and appreciate them. It pays. (How do you think you got that big bonus check, huh?)

For your consideration:

1. You mail a newsletter monthly, your upline mails one monthly, and the home office mails one monthly. Now your distributors receive three communications monthly. Do you think this could motivate and focus your group?

2. Do you read and look forward to your upline's newsletter?

3. What else can you put in your newsletter to make it more interesting? How can you better promote your products and opportunity?

Extra income has more value

Don't minimize the value of the extra income you earn from multilevel.

Distributor Joe's newest distributor, Jerry, was excited. "You won't believe this Joe, but today I received my first bonus check. Guess how much it is?"

Jerry was just starting. His check couldn't be very much. "What should I say?" thought Joe. "I don't want to embarrass him by guessing too low."

"Aw, come on Joe, take a guess," pleaded Jerry.

"Okay. I'd guess about $100."

"Pretty close. My check is $90! This is the best thing that ever happened to me."

Joe couldn't understand why Jerry was so excited. Certainly $90 wasn't going to change the world.

Jerry continued, "My take home pay is only $900 a month. Do you know what this $90 represents?"

"About a 10% increase, right?" guessed Joe.

"No, no, no. You don't understand at all. Each month after rent, car payment, food, bills, etc., I'm left with about $9 spending money that I can call my own. This $90 check increases my spending money by TEN TIMES."

Not everyone needs the big checks to get excited. Sometimes as leaders we forget how important the small bonus checks can be.

Why not incorporate the "spendable income" concept into your recruiting presentations? Most people can relate to a small increase in spendable income.

Talent isn't necessary

A young man wanted to know the secret of success. His business had recently failed. His spouse, relatives, and in-laws pleaded with him to quit dreaming and get a good solid 9-to-5 job.

The young man made an appointment with the richest man in his city. "Please, please tell me the secret of your success. Is it a special talent? Is it knowledge? What made you successful?"

The rich man smiled. "Let me tell you a story."

"The first time I tried going into business for myself, I failed miserably. The second business I tried failed before I even started. The third business I mismanaged. I thought that you needed a 50% success ratio to succeed. I was wrong."

The young man asked, "Do you mean you have to do better than 50% right?"

"No," continued the rich man, "you hardly ever have to be right. I failed in 19 consecutive businesses. On the average, I lost $1,000 per try, or a total of $19,000. On my twentieth attempt, I succeeded for the first time. The profits in the first year were over $100,000. So you see, I lost $19,000 on 19 mistakes, and made $100,000 on my first success. You can be wrong and fail 19 out of 20 times and still succeed!"

The young man smiled. "You don't have to be smart, knowledgeable, or talented to succeed. You just have to be persistent. You can be wrong 95% of the time and it still won't keep you from success."

Do you have distributors who quit at the first disappointment? Do your friends and relatives discourage you from trying again?

Have courage. Don't quit. You only have to have one success. When you are rich and famous, everyone forgets your 19 mistakes. Why? Your 19 mistakes won't matter as long as you continue to reach for your success.

If you never do anything, you won't make a mistake. Is that what you want for your life? Of course not. Get started making some mistakes so success will come your way.

Action pays more than study

Once upon a time, a genius was born. This young man showed exceptional intelligence from a very early age. At age five, he could speak 15 different languages. At age seven, he could name every country in the world and its capital. At age 12, he memorized the entire New York City phone book. His reputation grew as he demonstrated his knowledge throughout the United States.

Finally, at age 21, his feats of knowledge were so popular that the President of the United States granted him and his agent an appointment. The young man gave a fabulous demonstration of accumulated knowledge. When finished, his agent said, "Mr. President. No one in America has accumulated as much knowledge as this young man. He would be a true asset as a consultant to your cabinet. How much would you pay to have him on staff?

The president thought for a moment and said, "About $300."

"Is that $300 a day or $300 per hour?" asked the agent.

The president answered, "$300 for life. Everything this young man knows is in a $300 set of encyclopedias."

What is more important? Knowledge or results? Knowledge is easy to obtain. Results require work.

Distributors fall into the trap of confusing pleasant activity with results. They'll say, "I've really been busy this week. I've read two nutrition books, listened to the leadership cassette series, and attended a motivational seminar. I'm really growing as a person and as a distributor."

Bunk!

These distributors hide behind a quest for knowledge so they won't have to face prospects in the real world of multilevel. You'll see the same distributors at every meeting, seminar, and rally. They make sure they have no time to recruit or sell; they are too busy learning!

How many times have you seen a new, untrained distributor lead your group's production with just his raw enthusiasm? Knowledge? Well, if his prospects need to know something, he can look it up or call his sponsor.

What can you do with your distributors that hide in meetings and seminars? Set some two-on-one appointments and take them with you. Don't wait for them to set the appointments. Eternity will come first. Sponsor a new distributor or two into their group. Help them overcome their fear and catch fire by making the presentations while they watch. The results? Two things can happen.

First, your professional student could get excited and start working the business. You've given him a little confidence by helping him build his group.

Or second, your distributor will continue to be a professional seminar attendee. But it's not all bad. At least the new distributors you sponsored will have someone to call for information.

More dangers of overtraining

A middle-aged man had worked as the school's janitor for 25 years. Today, the school superintendent called him into his office.

"I've looked at your original application from 25 years ago. It says here you never went to college. Is that right?"

The janitor replied, "That's correct. I never attended college."

"Your application doesn't show that you graduated from high school. Did you attend high school?"

"No. I never attended high school."

"I'm sorry to tell you this, but the school board has a new policy. All school employees must have at least a high school diploma. For 25 years you have done a terrific job, but I have to let you go. Rules are rules."

The janitor turned in his mop and went home. "What can I do? I've been a janitor all my life. Maybe I can start my own janitorial business."

The first company he contacted said, "Sure, you can do the clean-up here. I remember how you did such a great job at the school."

The next company said the same thing. Soon the janitor had more buildings to clean than he could personally do. He hired an assistant.

Business continued to grow. Soon the janitor hired more employees. His customers were so happy with his work that they gave him additional small construction contracts.

After a couple of years, the janitor became quite wealthy. He had dozens of employees, trucks, equipment, and a six figure bank account.

Then, one day he received a letter to come down to his bank. The vice president greeted the janitor and said, "It's a pleasure to have you come down to our bank. We've never seen you here. Your employees always make your deposits. We checked our old records and found that you never signed the signature card to open your bank account. Could you sign it for us now, just to keep our records straight?"

The janitor replied, "I don't know how to write. You see, I've never been to school. Would an X be okay?"

"Sure. No problem." The banker didn't want to offend his largest customer. "This is amazing! Here you are, a janitor, who has succeeded in business and become our biggest account. Just think what you could have achieved with an education!"

"Heck!" said the janitor. "If I had an education, I'd still be a janitor!"

Developing leaders

The flood continued to get worse. The water rose from the river banks and demolished the town. On the outskirts of town, on high ground, lived Darrell.

Would the flood waters reach Darrell's house? Should he sandbag the perimeter? "No need to worry," said Darrell, "I'll say a prayer and ask for God's protection. I'm sure everything will be all right."

The waters continued to rise. Soon, water covered the first floor of the house. Darrell simply went upstairs and stared out the window.

A boat floated by with the civil defense rescue team. "Hey Darrell, need a ride to safety? The flood is getting worse."

"No problem," said Darrell. "I'm on high ground, plus I said a prayer. Just go on without me. I'll be all right."

The flood did get worse. The water filled the second story, so he climbed onto the roof. Darrell said another quick prayer asking for God's protection.

A helicopter flew over the house. The pilot yelled through the loudspeaker, "Darrell! Climb up into my helicopter. The flood is getting worse."

"Don't worry about me. I've got things under control." As the helicopter flew away, the flood waters continued to rise.

Soon the water was up to Darrell's neck - then over his head - and then it was over. Darrell perished in the flood.

Darrell led a good life, so it was no surprise that he went straight to heaven. St. Peter gave him the grand tour and introduced him to God.

"You know, God, heaven's great," Darrell said, "but I didn't want to get here so fast. I still wanted to do some good works on earth, but then that flood came. I used to think you were a great guy and listened to my prayers, but after that flood wiped me out, I wonder. Don't you listen to the prayers of your faithful on earth? Don't you remember me asking you for safety?"

God replied, "Hey, I sent a helicopter and a boat."

Do you have distributors who expect you to do everything? Have you been hearing requests like this?

"Could you call this prospect for me? He's not interested but I thought maybe you could convince him."

"My distributor has some appointments and I can't make them. Would you work with him?"

"Don't mail me the products. Couldn't you bring them over to my house? It would save postage."

"I don't have time to recruit. Would you put a few distributors in my downline to get me started?"

"It's so far to those meetings. Since you'll be there anyway, would you see if I have any guests show up?"

"My distributor has so many product questions. I thought it would be best if he got the answers straight from you."

Tired of holding up the world on your shoulders? Maybe you should look at your group. Is your group made up of distributors looking to you for leadership? Or, do you have leaders that build without your day-to-day support?

The secret of building a large distributor organization is to build a few leaders. You can't do it all yourself. *The measure of a successful multilevel organization is the number of leaders, not the number of distributors.*

Which would you rather have in your organization: three good leaders or 100 dependent distributors? Distributors may come and go, but leaders will build distributor organizations.

How does one build leaders? With a lot of hard work. That's why there are so few leaders. Here is a quick step-by-step program for leadership development.

1. Develop him yourself.

Wouldn't it be easier to steal a multilevel leader from another company? In the short run – yes. In the long run – no. Consider this: a leader leaves his present sponsor and company because you made a better offer. Won't this same leader leave you when someone else makes an even better offer? Then what will you have left? Zero. Temporary leaders have the same value as a dependent distributor.

Your best leaders will be home-grown. They will be loyal to you, their mentor, because you took the time to train them and develop their skills. They won't jump to the next greatest and best deal. Why should they leave for the unknown when they have guaranteed success with you?

2. Look for desire

Don't worry about a person's present skill level. You want to develop a person with a strong desire, someone who won't quit when the going gets tough. There are millions of people with skills who have dead end jobs. Why? They don't have the desire to go further. You don't want to waste your time with a quitter.

So, look for the distributor with the burning desire to succeed.

3. Move in

Maybe not change residences, but plan to spend every possible moment working together. Travel together to meetings and trainings. Recruit as a team. Teach your future leader everything you know. It may take six months or even a year, but you want your future leader to have every piece of knowledge and skill you possess.

Are you willing to invest six months or a year developing one leader? Some multilevel distributors have worked for years and never developed a leader. They wonder why they never get ahead. They failed to invest their time and energy into developing leaders.

When finished, your new leader should outshine your performance. Why? Not only does he know everything you do, but he also has his own personal information and skills. Don't worry about being jealous. It's hard to be mad at a downline leader building a larger organization than you. Wouldn't you want 10 downline leaders outshining your performance? Your bonus check should soothe any ego problems you may have.

4. Enjoy

When you develop leaders, you can enjoy multilevel. If you take a vacation, your business will continue to grow. Meetings will continue. New distributors will continue to join. Your leaders will continue working independent of your efforts, coaching or motivation. They are working for themselves, not you.

Compare that scenario with distributors who don't build leaders. They spend their vacations phoning their dependent downliners, begging, cajoling, pleading for activity. These distributors are sentenced to a lifetime of frustration, trying to build a business by themselves.

What's the bottom line?

Support your distributors but work with your leaders.

"Knock, knock."

"Who's there?"

"Opportunity."

"Can't be. Opportunity only knocks once."

The restaurant

The sponsor was reassuring his prospect.

"Do you know anything about running a restaurant?"

"No."

"Let's say you wanted to open your own restaurant, but wanted to do it slowly. You aren't sure you can handle it, so you decide to open only one day a week, Friday. You won't take any risks. Your restaurant will be strictly part time, open only two hours on Friday evenings."

"I could feel comfortable with that."

"To make things easier, you should allow customers to come by invitation only. You don't want too many on your first night. I will help you for the first couple of Fridays."

"So far this sounds easy enough."

"We'll invite just four of your friends for opening night. You and I will serve their meals. If they like the food, we'll ask them to tell others."

"Sounds fair."

"The next Friday night, we will allow each of your four friends to bring one new guest. Now we have 8 customers. You and I have last week's experience under our belt, so we should be a little better now, right?"

"Sure. Eight people wouldn't be any problem for you and me."

"The next Friday night, we will allow each of our eight customers to bring one additional guest. Now we have 16 guests to serve. We still plan to be open only two hours and keep this business part-time, so maybe we'll expand to another night. We don't want more than 16 guests at a time."

"That makes sense."

"Let's expand to Tuesday nights. We'll hire our most enthusiastic customer as an assistant and begin to train him to do the same. So our Friday nights stay easy to operate, we'll send some of our customers to Tuesday nights. This will help Tuesdays start with a bang."

"I'm getting the picture. I can learn as I go. Maybe multilevel won't be so hard if I go one step at a time. Sign me up. Let's start inviting my four guests for my Friday night opportunity meeting."

The biggest fear new prospects have is the fear of the unknown. We can use the restaurant story to assure them they can learn, one step at a time.

For a free newsletter and catalog of other KAAS Publishing books, write us at:

KAAS Publishing
P.O. Box 890084
Houston, TX 77289

or call us at

(713) 280-9800

Here are three more *Big Al* Recruiting Books you'll want in your library:

#1 *Big Al Tells All, The Recruiting System (Sponsoring Magic).* This is the original *Big Al* classic that details the entire *Big Al* Recruiting System. You'll learn about:

- Locating and qualifying new prospects
- Closing before you start your presentation
- The magic two questions
- Making fear of loss work for you
- The dairy farm syndrome
- The 25-minute presentation that works
- Strawberries as a selling tool
- Ridding your organization of the ten deadly myths
- And much, much more

If you were to read only one *Big Al* book, this should be your first choice.

#2 *How To Create A Recruiting Explosion.* This book contains more advanced recruiting techniques such as:

- Locating the fishing hole
- Too good to be true
- The checklist close
- Trade show challenges
- Finding the best people
- Ad techinques
- Handling questions
- Street smarts
- Office problems

And, the all-time blockbuster recruiting technique, *The Stair Step Solution!*

#4 *How To Build MLM Leaders For Fun & Profit.* Build massive downline organizations by building independent, motivated leaders. Your group is only as strong as its leaders. Special sections on:

- Cloning superhuman leaders
- The $93,000 Recruiting System
- Piggy-back your opportunity
- Ninja mail
- The file drawer method
- Hype from the top
- The 2% myth
- How to get all the prospects you want
- Streamline your business
- *Man Kills Family Pet* principle
- And, much, much, more

Just pick from the many easy methods and systems to build your leader network fast.

Volume Discounts

All *Big Al* Recruiting Books are $12.95 each. For the professional leader who wishes to take advantage of *Big Al's* surprisingly generous quantity discounts, the following schedule applies for any combination of his four books:

10-24	6.95 ea.
25-49	6.00 ea.
50-99	5.00 ea.
100-499	4.25 ea.
500 or more	3.95 ea.

Never been to a "live", hands-on *Big Al* recruiting workshop? Here's your chance. Almost three hours on audio cassettes of special *Big Al* recruiting applications that will help you build your downline faster. This workshop was recorded live in London, England in 1991. Get the inside methods that top MLM pros use to build large bonus checks. The entire workshop can be ordered by sending $19.95 to:

KAAS Publishing
P.O. Box 890084
Houston, TX 77289
or order by credit card by calling
(713) 280-9800